WITCH BREW

Spooky verse for Hallowe'en

Chosen by Zenka and Ian Woodward

Beaver Books

For
Tricia and Dawn Simmonds
With love

A Beaver Original
Published by Arrow Books Limited
17–21 Conway Street, London W1P 6JD
A division of the Hutchinson Publishing Group
London Melbourne Sydney Auckland Johannesburg
and agencies throughout the world

First published 1984

Set in Linoterm Bembo by
JH Graphics Limited, Reading, Berks
Printed and bound in Great Britain by
Anchor Brendon Limited, Tiptree, Essex

ISBN 0 09 935360 1

There are witches about . . .
something is brewing

Over the waters and on the wind,
Come witches flying of every kind,
On goats and boars and bears and cats,
Some upon broomsticks, some like bats,
Howling, hurtling, hurrying, all,
Come to the tree at the master's call.

Dom Piccini

Witches, as we usually know them, were women thought to have made a contract to serve evil spirits. This contract was usually sealed with blood. In return for their promise they were given power to do things beyond the abilities of ordinary people.

Most people today laugh at the very mention of witchcraft. Yet the belief which folk once had in the supernatural powers of witches remains very strong in some places even now.

In olden days it was believed that witches could bring sickness and death to anybody they wished. They could go through locked doors. They could ride through the air on broom sticks. They could transform themselves into animals.

To enable her to do all these things the witch had at her disposal a great amount of apparatus – objects made with magical secrecy. She concocted fiendish numbers and formulas. She prepared herbs and brews, rare juices and liquids, blood and milk, adding deadly poisonous plants like mandrake. She also used mystic diagrams and geometric figures and wonder-making circles and pentacles.

It was said that the witches' greatest delight was to bring harm and suffering to those whom they did not like. Sometimes they would make small waxen or clay figures of those they wished to harm or kill. They would then prick these images or slowly melt them in the hope and belief that this would cause suffering and eventual death to the persons represented by the figures.

At certain times of the year it was believed that there were great gatherings of witches. These were known as witches' sabbaths. Here they met with the Devil and performed elaborate ceremonies.

The power of names forms a branch of almost all witchcraft. The name was considered to be a part of a man. So, by pronouncing it under proper magical conditions, he could be influenced for either good or bad.

Gods and spirits were believed to have special magic names, known only to a chosen few. Uttering these names was supposed to give a man power over these supernatural beings. In this way there grew up the spells and charms which form so large a part of magic, and many examples of these have been included in this book.

Charm-words, secret sentences called incantations, or sometimes magical objects were used to summon up the spirits of the dead or goblins and fairies, who would then obey the orders of the one who possessed the secret. The curse is part of such a belief.

Wherever a belief in magic existed, there too could be found the special magician or sorcerer. They were known under all sorts of names: wizard, necromancer, witch, conjurer, medicine-man, astrologer and soothsayer. And, because they were believed to enjoy unusual powers over the spirit world or could foretell the future or read the secrets of the past, they were regarded everywhere with fearful respect.

To many educated people today, however, the strangest thing about witchcraft and magic is that anyone could possibly believe it. But scientists are just beginning to discover how, and how much, a person is affected by *his own mind*. If a man believes in magic and a spell is cast on him, he will probably 'go along' with the spell.

The old name of All Hallows (for the festival of All Saints) survives in Hallowe'en or All Hallows Eve – the wonderful, magical, creepy night of 31st October. The curious customs associated with Hallowe'en come down to us today from an odd mixture of pagan and Christian traditions.

For instance, when children eat apples and nuts on that evening, or pick up apples floating in a tub of water with their teeth, they are following the custom of the pagan Romans –

for Hallowe'en coincides with the ancient Roman festival which honours Pomona, goddess of fruits and gardens. The Christian church, on the other hand, celebrates the feast of All Saints on 1st November, and the following day is therefore called All Saints' Day, when the faithful remember the spiritual union of dead and living.

It was because many people did not understand the true meaning of the Church's 'union of souls' that there arose the superstition that ghosts appeared at Hallowe'en or could be easily conjured up then. We have done our best to invoke in these pages our own congregation of ghosts, hauntings and creepily bewitched monsters.

On Hallowe'en witches are said to be out on their broomsticks and mischievous elves, goblins and fairies are abroad too. At Hallowe'en parties chestnuts are roasted, an omen being traced in every pop and leap. And, to add to the spine-chilling atmosphere at Hallowe'en, many children make grotesque lanterns out of hollowed-out turnips.

So, make haste – there are witches about! And more besides. In the following pages we have assembled our own Hallowe'en . . . just for you. There are charms and curses, spells and enchantments, many of them enacted in shadowy churchyards whiplashed by thunder and lightning.

Here lurks – well, who knows what? Certainly, within magic woods and haunted houses you will find strange midnight beasts with equally weird names, such as Bogus-boo, Gombeen, Multikertwigo, Horny Goloch, Sniggle and Demon Manchanda. Other eerie creatures of the blackest nights scurry through this book, including bewitched screech-owls, witches' black cats and the ugly, squelching Malfeasance.

You will find birds doomed to Hell, the Devil or Dark Angel himself, ghouls and ogres, elves, goblins, changelings, nymphs and fairies and the old hags – the witches. They are all here with one terrible aim in mind: to trouble our sleep and scare us half to death! So, happy, scary reading, and –

From witches and wizards and longtailed
    buzzards,
And creeping things that run in hedge bottoms,
Good Lord deliver us!

Zenka and Ian Woodward

7

Prelude to the witches' brew

Hey-how for Hallowe'en,
All the witches to be seen;
Some black and some green;
Hey-how for Hallowe'en!

Unknown

Next . . . the witches' delight

God's plan made a hopeful beginning,
But man spoiled his chances by sinning.
  We trust that God's glory
  Will end up the story,
But at present the other side's winning!

Unknown

Now it is the time of night

Now it is the time of night,
  That the graves, all gaping wide,
Every one lets forth his sprite,
  In the churchway paths to glide:
And we fairies, that do run
  By the triple Hecate's team,
From the presence of the sun,
  Following darkness like a dream,
Now are frolic.

William Shakespeare

Nasty night

Whose are the hands you hear
Pulling the roof apart?
What stamps its hoof
Between the bedroom ceiling and the slates?

Roy Fuller

This night

This night, as I sit here alone,
And brood on what is dead and gone,
The owl that's in this Highgate Wood
Has found his fellow in my mood;
To every star, as it doth rise –
Oh–o–o! Oh–o–o! he shivering cries.

And, looking at the Moon this night,
There's that dark shadow in her light.
Ah! Life and Death, my fairest one,
Thy lover is a skeleton!
'And why is that?' I question – 'why?'
Oh–o–o! Oh–o–o! the owl doth cry.

W. H. Davies

The bird of night

A shadow is floating
   through the moonlight,
Its wings don't make a sound.
Its claws are long, its beak is bright.
Its eyes try all the corners of the night.

It calls and calls: all the air swells and heaves
And washes up and down like water.
The ear that listens to the owl believes
In death. The bat beneath the eaves,

The mouse beneath the stone are still as death.
The owl's air washes them like water.
The owl goes back and forth inside the night,
And the night holds its breath.

Randall Jarrell

To-whit to-who

When icicles hang by the wall,
   And Dick the shepherd blows his nail,
And Tom bears logs into the hall,
   And milk comes frozen home in pail;
When blood is nipped, and ways be foul,
Then nightly sings the staring owl:
     To-whit to-who,
     A merry note,
While greasy Joan does keel the pot.*

When all aloud the wind does blow,
   And coughing drowns the parson's saw;
And birds sit brooding in the snow,
   And Marian's nose looks red and raw;
When roasted crabs hiss in the bowl,
Then nightly sings the staring owl:
     To-whit to-who,
     A merry note,
While greasy Joan does keel the pot.

William Shakespeare

* Keel = cool

My cats
(*A witch speaks*)

I like to toss him up and down
A heavy cat weighs half a crown
With a hey do diddle my cat Brown.

I like to pinch him on the sly
When nobody is passing by
With a hey do diddle my cat Fry.

I like to ruffle up his pride
And watch him skip and turn aside
With a Hey do diddle my cat Hyde.

Hey Brown and Fry and Hyde my cats
That sit on tombstones for your mats.

Stevie Smith

Noises in the night

Midnight's bell goes ting, ting, ting, ting, ting,
Then dogs do howl, and not a bird does sing
But the nightingale, and she goes twit, twit,
    twit.
Owls then on every bough do sit,
Ravens croak on chimney tops,
The cricket in the chamber hops,
And the cats cry mew, mew, mew.
The nibbling mouse is not asleep,
But he goes peep, peep, peep, peep, peep.
    And the cats cry mew, mew, mew,
    And still the cats cry mew, mew, mew.

Thomas Middleton

The Malfeasance

It was a dark, dank, dreadful night
And while millions were abed
The Malfeasance bestirred itself
And raised its ugly head.

The leaves dropped quietly in the night,
In the sky Orion shone;
The Malfeasance bestirred itself
Then crawled around till dawn.

Taller than a chimney stack,
More massive than a church,
It slithered to the city
With a purpose and a lurch.

Squelch, squelch, the scaly feet
Flapped along the roads;
Nothing like it had been seen
Since a recent fall of toads.

Bullets bounced off the beast,
Aircraft made it grin;
Its open mouth made an eerie sound
Uglier than sin.

Still it floundered forwards,
Still the city reeled;
There was panic on the pavements,
Even policemen squealed.

Then suddenly someone suggested
(As the beast had done no harm)
It would be kinder to show it kindness,
Better to stop the alarm.

When they offered it refreshment
The creature stopped in its track;
When they waved a greeting to it
Steam rose from its back.

As the friendliness grew firmer
The problem was quietly solved:
Terror turned to triumph and
The Malfeasance dissolved.

And where it stood there hung a mist,
And in its wake a shining trail,
And the people found each other
And thereby hangs a tail.

Alan Bold

Thunder and lightning

Blood punches through every vein
As Lightning strips the windowpane.

Under its flashing whip, a white
Village leaps to light.

On tubs of thunder, fists of rain
Slog it out of sight again.

Blood punches the heart with fright
As rain belts the village night.

James Kirkup

On a night of snow

Cat, if you go outdoors you must walk in the
   snow.
You will come back with little white shoes on
   your feet,
Little white slippers of snow that have heels of
   sleet.
Stay by the fire, my Cat. Lie still, do not go.
See how the flames are leaping and hissing low;
I will bring you a saucer of milk like a
   marguerite,
So white and so smooth, so spherical and so
   sweet—
Stay with me, Cat. Outdoors the wild winds
   blow.

Outdoors the wild winds blow, Mistress, and
   dark is the night.
Strange voices cry in the trees, intoning strange
   lore;
And more than cats move, lit by our eyes' green
   light,
On silent feet where the meadow grasses hang
   hoar—
Mistress, there are portents abroad of magic
   and might,
And things that are yet to be done. Open the
   door!

Elizabeth Coatsworth

The Bogus-boo

The Bogus-boo
Is a creature who
Comes out at night – and why?
He likes the air;
He likes to scare
The nervous passer-by

Out from the park
At dead of dark
He comes with huffling pad.
If, when alone,
You hear his moan,
'Tis like to drive you mad.

He has two wings,
Pathetic things,
With which he cannot fly.
His tusks look fierce,
Yet could not pierce
The mearest butterfly.

He has six ears,
But what he hears
Is very faint and small;
And with the claws
On his eight paws
He cannot scratch at all.

He looks so wise
With his owl-eyes,
His aspect grim and ghoulish;
But truth to tell,
He sees not well
And is distinctly foolish.

This Bogus-boo,
What can he do
But huffle in the dark?
So don't take fright;
He has no bite
And very little bark.

James Reeves

Black

Black the angry colour,
The thunder colour,
The mourning colour,
The black dark underworld.
The creepy frightening colour,
Bare, black trees
Silhouetted against the sky.
The silent night robber
Creeping, creeping,
In the silent black night,
Doing his black deeds.
A fine black stallion
Streaking past.
The black, black darkness.
The raven–black hair,
The raven–black dress.
Black anger of the war,
The cold black damp caves
And the underground caverns.
The angry black cold sea
Reaching,
With its black fingers,
Throwing the forlorn ships
To their black
On the black rocks
In the black depths of the sea.
Black,
Black, the perilous colour
And black the serious colour.
Black,
The colour of the dead.

Jane Chester

Oft in the lone churchyard

Oft in the lone churchyard at night I've seen,
By glimpse of moon-shine chequering through
  the trees,
The school-boy with his satchel in his hand,
Whistling aloud to bear his courage up,
And lightly tripping over the long flat stones,
(With nettles skirted, and with moss
  overgrown),
That tell in homely phrase who lie below.
Sudden he starts, and hears, or thinks he hears,
The sound of something purring at his heels;
Full fast he flies, and dares not look behind him,
Till out of breath he overtakes his fellows,
Who gather round, and wonder at the tale
Of horrid apparition, tall and ghastly,
               That walks at dead of night,
                 or takes his stand
               Over some new-opened
                 grave; and (strange to tell!)
               Vanishes at crowing of the
                 cock.

Robert Blair

The witch

Weary went the old Witch,
Weary of her pack,
She sat her down by the churchyard wall,
And jerked it off her back.

The cord brake, yes, the cord brake,
Just where the dead did lie,
And Charms and Spells and Sorceries
Spilled out beneath the sky.

Weary was the old Witch;
She rested her old eyes
From the lantern-fruited yew trees,
And the scarlet of the skies;

And out the dead came stumbling,
From every rift and crack,
Silent as moss, and plundered
The gaping pack.

They wish them, three times over,
Away they skip full soon:
Bat and Mole and Leveret,
Under the rising moon;

Owl and Newt and Nightjar:
They take their shapes and creep
Silent as churchyard lichen,
While she squats asleep.

All of these dead were stirring:
Each unto each did call,
'A Witch, a Witch is sleeping
Under the churchyard wall;

'A Witch, a Witch is sleeping . . .'
The shrillness ebbed away;
And up the way-worn moon clomb bright,
Hard on the track of day.

She shone, high, wan, and silvery;
Day's colours paled and died:
And, save the mute and creeping worm,
Nought else was there beside.

Names may be writ; and mounds rise;
Purporting, Here be bones:
But empty is that churchyard
Of all save stones.

Owl and Newt and Nightjar,
Leveret, Bat, and Mole
Haunt and call in the twilight
Where she slept, poor soul.

Walter de la Mare

The little boy lost

The wood was rather old and dark
The witch was very ugly
And if it hadn't been for father
Walking there so smugly
I never should have followed
The beckoning of her finger.
Ah me how long ago it was
And still I linger
Under the ever interlacing beeches
Over a carpet of moss.
I lift my hand but it never reaches
To where the breezes toss
The sun-kissed leaves above.
The sun?
Beware.
The sun never comes here.
Round about and round I go
Up and down and to and fro,
The woodlouse hops upon the tree
Or should do but I really cannot see.
Happy fellow. Why can't I be
Happy as he?
The wood grows darker every day
It's now a bad place in a way
But I lost the way
Last Tuesday.
Did I love father, mother, home?
Not very much; but now they're gone
I think of them with kindly toleration
Bred inevitably of separation.

Really if I could find some food
I should be happy enough in this wood
But darker days and hungrier I must spend
Till hunger and darkness make an end.

Stevie Smith

Mother Maudlin the witch

Within a gloomy dimble she doth dwell
Down in a pit overgrown with brakes and
  briars,
Close by the ruins of a shaken abbey
Torn, with an earthquake, down unto the
  ground,
Among graves, and grots, near an old charnel
  house,
Where you shall find her sitting in her form,
As fearful, and melancholic, as that
She is about; with caterpillar's kells,
And knotty cobwebs, rounded in with spells;
Thence she steals forth to relief, in the fogs,
And rotten mists, upon the fens, and bogs,
Down to the drowned lands of Lincolnshire;
To make ewes cast their lambs. . . .

Ben Jonson

A country witch

There's that old hag Moll Brown,
  look, see, just past!
I wish the ugly sly old witch
Would tumble over in the ditch;
I wouldn't pick her out not very fast.
I don't think she's belied, it's as clear as the sun
That she's a witch if ever there was one.
Yes, I do know just hereabout of two
Or three folks that have learnt
  what Moll can do.
She did, one time, a pretty deal of harm
To Farmer Gruff's folks, down at Lower Farm.
One day, you know,
  they happened to offend her,
And not a little to their sorrow,
Because they would not give or lend her
The thing she came to beg or borrow;
And so, you know, they soon began to find
That she'd a-left her evil wish behind.

She soon bewitched them;
  and she had such power,
That she did make their milk and ale turn sour,
And addle all the eggs their fowls did lay;
They couldn't fetch the butter in the churn,
And cheeses soon began to turn
All back again to curds and whey.

The little pigs a-running with the sow
Did sicken somehow, nobody knew how,
And fall, and turn their snouts towards the sky,
And only give one little grunt and die;
And all the little ducks and chicken
Were death-struck while they were a-pickin'
Their food, and fell upon their head,
And flapped their wings
    and dropped down dead.

They couldn't fat the calves;
    they wouldn't thrive;
They couldn't save their lambs alive;
Their sheep all took the rot and gave no wool;
Their horses fell away to skin and bones,
And got so weak they couldn't pull
A half a peck of stones;
The dog got dead-alive and drowsy,
The cat fell sick and wouldn't mousey;
And if the wretched souls went up to bed
The hag did come and ride them all half dead.
They used to keep her out of the house it's true,
A-nailing up at door a horse's shoe;
And I've a-heard the farmer's wife did try
To drive a needly of a pin
In through her old hard withered skin
And draw her blood, a-coming by;
But she could never fetch a drop,
She bent the pin and broke the needle's top
Against her skin, you know, and that, of course,
Did only make the hag bewitch them worse!

William Barnes

Witches' charms

The weather is fair, the wind is good –
Up, dame, on your horse of wood!
Or else tuck up your grey frock,
And saddle your goat or your green cock,
And make his bridle a ball of thread
To roll up how many miles you have rid.
Quickly come away,
For we all stay.

The owl is abroad, the bat and the toad,
And so is the cat-a-mountain;
The ant and the mole sit both in a hole,
And the frog peeps out of the fountain,
The dogs they do bay, and the timbrels play.
The spindle is now a-turning;
The moon it is red, and the stars have fled,
But the sky is a-burning.

Ben Jonson

Hallowe'en

Witch's fiddle, turnip middle,
Scoop it all out with a spoon.
Curve mouth and eyes
With a careful knife
Beneath a Hallowe'en moon.

Witch–broom handle, long wax candle,
Stick spell–firm in the hole.
Find a match,
Step back and watch
Hushed as a Hallowe'en mole.

Witch–keen sight, strike bright light,
Match to the greasy wick.
See faint flame
Flick and falter,
Rise and stutter.
Part of the Hallowe'en game.

Witch–black cat; put turnip hat
Gently back on the top.
Turn out all moon.
Watch yellow eyes, mouth's flamed rays.
Hark for a Hallowe'en tune.

 For the witch's fiddle
 And the witch's cat
 And the crack
 Of a witch–broom handle
 Sing a haggard song
 On a moonless night
 To a turnip lantern candle.

John Kitching

All Hallowe'en

Witch and warlock all abroad
Revels keep by field and yard.

In the firelight of the farm
Boy and maiden one by one
Place their chestnuts in the grate
And for omens quietly wait;
To a string their apples tie,
Twirl them till they fallen lie;
Those whose fruits fall in a hurry,
They shall be the first to marry.

Witch and warlock all abroad
Revels keep by field and yard.

Apples from the beams hang down
To be caught by mouth alone,
Mugs of ale on Nut-Crack Night
And many a tale of ghost and sprite,
Come to cheer and chill the heart,
While the candles faint and start,
While the flickering firelight paints
Pictures of the hallowed saints.

Witch and warlock all abroad
Revels keep by field and yard.

Pauline Clarke

Punkie night
(or Hallowe'en)

It's punkie night, tonight,
It's punkie night, tonight,
Give us a candle, give us a light,
It's punkie night tonight.

Unknown

Hist whist

hist   whist
little ghostthings
tip–toe
twinkle–toe

little twitchy
witches and tingling
goblins
hob–a–nob   hob–a–nob

little hoppy happy
toad in tweeds
tweeds
little itchy mousies

with scuttling
eyes   rustle and run   and
hidehidehide
whisk

whisk   look out for the old woman
with the wart on her nose
what she'll do to yer
nobody knows

for she knows the devil   ooch
the devil   ouch
the devil
ach   the great

green
dancing
devil
devil

devil
devil

    wheeEEE

   e. e. cummings

Hallowe'en

On Hallowe'en the old ghosts come
About us, and they speak to some;
To others they are dumb.

They haunt the hearts that loved them best;
In some they are by grief possessed,
In other hearts they rest.

They have a knowledge they would tell;
To some of us it is a knell,
To some, a miracle.

They come unseen and go unseen;
And some will never know they've been,
And some will know all they mean.

              Eleanor Farjeon

The witches' call

Come, witches, come, on your hithering
  brooms!
The moorland is dark and still –
Over church and the churchyard tombs
To the oakwood under the hill.
Come through the mist and wandering cloud,
Fly with the crescent moon;
Come where the witches and warlocks crowd,
Come soon . . . soon!

Leave your room with its shadowy cat,
Your cauldron over the hearth;
Seize your cloak and pointed hat,
Come by the witches' path.
Float from the earth like a rising bird,
Stream through the darkening air,
Come at the sound of our secret word,
Come to the witches' lair!

Clive Sansom

The witches' song

'I have been all day looking after
A raven feeding upon a quarter;
And, soon as she turned her back to the south,
I snatched this morsel out of her mouth.'

'I last night lay all alone
On the ground, to hear the mandrake groan;
And plucked him up, though he grew full low:
And, as I had done, the cock did crow.'

'And I had been plucking (plants among)
Hemlock, henbane, adder's-tongue,
Nightshade, moonwort, libbard's-bane;
And twice by the dogs was like to be ta'en.'

'Yes, I have brought, to help your vows,
Horned poppy, cypress boughs.
The fig-tree wild, that grows on tombs,
And juice that from the larch-tree comes,
The basilisk's blood, and the viper's skin;
And now our orgies let's begin.'

Ben Jonson

A witch's song

Now I'm furnished for the flight,
Now I go, now I fly,
Malkin my sweet spirit and I.
Oh, what a dainty pleasure it is
To ride in the air
When the moon shines fair,
And sing and dance and toy and kiss.
Over woods, high rocks and mountains,
Over seas, our mistress's fountains,
Over steeples, towers, and turrets,
We fly by night, among troops of spirits.
No ring of bells to our ears sounds,
No howls of wolves, no yelp of hounds.
No, not the noise of water's breach,
Or cannon's throat can our height reach.

Thomas Middleton

Another witch's song

I from the jaws of a gardener's bitch
Did snatch these bones, and then leapt the ditch:
Yet went I back to the house again,
Killed the black cat, and here is the brain.

I went to the toad, breeds under the wall,
I charmed him out, and he came at my call;
I scratched out the eyes of the owl before;
I tore the bat's wing: what would you have
    more?

Ben Jonson

Dame Hickory

'Dame Hickory, Dame Hickory,
Here's sticks for your fire,
Furze–twigs, and oak–twigs,
And beech–twigs, and briar!'
But when old Dame Hickory came for to see,
She found 'twas the voice of the False Faërie.

'Dame Hickory, Dame Hickory,
Here's meat for your broth,
Goose–flesh, and hare's flesh,
And pig's trotters both!'
But when old Dame Hickory came for to see,
She found 'twas the voice of the False Faërie.

'Dame Hickory, Dame Hickory,
Here's a wolf at your door,
His teeth grinning white,
And his tongue wagging sore!'
'Nay!' said Dame Hickory, 'ye False Faërie!'
But a wolf 'twas indeed, and famished was he.

'Dame Hickory, Dame Hickory,
Here's buds for your tomb,
Bramble, and lavender,
And rosemary bloom!'
'Whsst!' sighs Dame Hickory, 'you False
    Faërie,
You cry like a wolf, you do, and trouble poor
    me.'

Walter de la Mare

The Egg-shell

The wind took off with the sunset —
The fog came up with the tide,
When the Witch of the North took an Egg-shell
With a little Blue Devil inside.
'Sink,' she said, 'or swim,' she said,
'It's all you will get from me.
And that is the finish of *him*!' she said,
And the Egg-shell went to sea.

The wind fell dead with the midnight —
The fog shut down like a sheet,
When the Witch of the North heard the Egg-
    shell
Feeling by hand for a fleet.
'Get!' she said, 'or you're gone,' she said,
But the little Blue Devil said 'No!'
'The sights are just coming on,' he said,
And he let the Whitehead go.

The wind got up with the morning —
The fog blew off with the rain,
When the Witch of the North saw the Egg-shell
And the little Blue Devil again.
'Did you swim?' she said. 'Did you sink?' she
    said,
And the little Blue Devil replied:
'For myself I swam, but I *think*,' he said,
'There's somebody sinking outside.'

Rudyard Kipling

A moon-witch

A moon-witch is no joke.
She comes as a sort of smoke.
She wisps in through the keyhole and feels
  about
Like a spider's arm or a smoke-elephant's snout
Till she finds her victim.
He collapses like a balloon – she has sucked him
Empty in a flash. Her misty feeler
Blooms red as blood in water, then milkily
  paler –
And fades. And a hundred miles off
She disguises her burp with a laugh.

Also she has a sort of electronic
Rocket-homing trick – and that is chronic.
She steals the signature
Of whoever she wants to bewitch
And swallows it. Now wherever he might be
He sees her face, horrible with evil glee,
Hurtling at him like a rocket – WHOP!
People see him stop.

He staggers, he smooths his brow, he is
  astonished –
Whatever it was, it seems to have vanished.

He doesn't know what he's in for.
He's done for.

Only deep in sleep he dreams and groans
A pack of hyenas are fighting over his bones.

In a week, he dies. Then 'Goodness!' the witch
  says,
And yawns and falls asleep for about ten days –
Like a huge serpent that just ate
Something its own weight.

Ted Hughes

Ghosts' stories

That bull-necked blotch-faced farmer from
  Drumlore
would never dream (or so we heard him boast
to neighbours at the lamb sales in
  Kirkcudbright)
of paying the least attention to a ghost.

Were we to blame for teaching him a lesson?
We wooed his daughter, spaded all his ewes,
brought a blight on his barley, drew the sea
rampaging over his sod. . .

If we had any doubt that he deserved it,
that went when we heard him stamp his ruined
  acres
and blame it all on God.

When we went on and frightened Miss
   McQueen
for keeping children in on Hallowe'en,
and wailed all night in the schoolhouse, she,
   poor woman,
sent for the Fire Brigade.
And so we made
fire lick from her hair, till they put her out.

The children knew what it was all about.

Alastair Reid

Hallowe'en night fright

Hallowe'en. She dressed up in a sheet,
A paper crown, a tail, a fierce expression,
High–button shoes, not fitting, on her feet,
A broken mask, her proudest child–possession,
A lantern on the handle of a broom,
While over the sky of her anticipation,
Shining and far away though in that room,
Feet, lantern, hands leapt like a constellation.
Outdoors she waved her lantern in wild daring
And yelled at a stranger passing in the night,
Half to cheer herself and half in play.
But scared herself with her own sudden
    scaring,
And ran from what she thought would run
    away,
And found she could not even frighten fright.

Paul Engle

42

My granny is a witch

I'm a very small boy
and my granny is a witch
I love my granny very much
but she's a witch.
Once on a summer night
she got up and went into the kitchen
I crept after her
and there was a strong smell of onions
up hopped granny on to the frying-pan
and burst out singing ever so loud
and I was ever so frightened
she beckoned to me
and together we flew out of the window
I held on as hard as I could
because the earth below was like a cup
peacocks were strutting over it
and swans swam all in white
it glittered like a Christmas tree
and we dropped into a cake shop
Granny stole some tarts
and I ate them
and Granny ate even more
because she was very tired
and then we came back on a pony
we got undressed ever so quietly
and slipped into bed
Granny told me not to make a noise.
Granny's very kind
it's a pity she's a witch though.

Arkady Mikhailov

The witch stepmother

'I was but seven year old
    When my mother she did die;
My father married the very worst woman
    The world did ever see.

For she has made me the loathly worm
    That lies at the foot of the tree,
And my sister Maisry she's made
    The mackerel of the sea.

And every Saturday at noon
    The mackerel comes to me,
And she takes my loathly head
    And lays it on her knee,
She combs it with a silver comb,
    And washes it in the sea.

Seven knights have I slain,
    Since I lay at the foot of the tree,
And were you not my own father,
    The eighth one you should be.'

The father sent for his lady,
    As fast as send could he:
'Where is my son that you sent from me,
    And my daughter Lady Maisry?'

'Your son is at our king's court,
    Serving for meat and fee;
And your daughter's at our queen's court,
    A waiting-woman is she.'

'You lie, you ill woman,
  So loud I hear you lie:
My son's the loathly worm,
  That lies at the foot of the tree,
And my daughter Lady Maisry
  Is the mackerel of the sea!'

She has taken a silver wand,
  And given him strokes three,
And he's started up the bravest knight
  That ever your eyes did see.

She has taken a small horn,
  And loud and shrill blew she,
And all the fish came unto her
  But the proud mackerel of the sea:
'You shaped me once an unseemly shape
  You shall never more shape me.'

He has sent to the wood
  For whins and for hawthorn,
And he has taken that gay lady
  And there he did her burn.

                                    Unknown

A witch's chant

Thou art weary, weary, weary,
　　Thou art weary and far away,
Hear me, gentle spirit, hear me,
　　Come before the dawn of day.

I hear a small voice from the hill,
The vapour is deadly, pale, and still –
A murmuring sigh is in the wood,
And the witching star is red as blood.

And in the cleft of heaven I scan
The giant form of a naked man;
His eye is like the burning brand,
And he holds a sword in his right hand.

All is not well. By dint of spell,
Somewhere between the heaven and hell
There is this night a wild deray:
The spirits have wandered from their way.

The purple drops shall tinge the moon
As she wanders through the midnight noon;
And the dawning heaven shall all be red
With blood by guilty angels shed.

Be as it will, I have the skill
To work by good or work by ill;
Then here's for pain, and here's for thrall,
And here's for conscience, worst of all.

Another chant, and then, and then,
Spirits shall come on Christian men –
Come from the earth, the air, or the sea,
Great Gil-Moules, I cry to thee!

Sleepest thou, wakest thou, lord of the wind,
Mount thy steeds and gallop them blind;
And the long-tailed fiery dragon outfly,
The rocket of heaven, the bomb of the sky.

Over the dog-star, over the wain,
Over the cloud, and the rainbow's mane,
Over the mountain, and over the sea,
    Haste – haste – haste to me!

Then here's for trouble, and here's for smart,
And here's for the pang that seeks the heart;
Here's for madness, and here's for thrall,
And here's for conscience, the worst of all!

James Hogg

The making of a charm
(from *Macbeth*)

First Witch: Round about the cauldron go;
    In the poisoned entrails throw.
    Toad, that under cold stone
    Days and night has thirty-one
    Sweltered venom sleeping got,
    Boil thou first in the charmed
        pot.

All:	Double, double toil and trouble; Fire, burn; and, cauldron, bubble.
Second Witch:	Fillet of a fenny snake, In the cauldron boil and bake; Eye of newt, and toe of frog, Wool of bat, and tongue of dog, Adder's fork, and blind-worm's sting, Lizard's leg, and howlet's wing— For a charm of powerful trouble, Like a hell-broth boil and bubble.
All:	Double, double toil and trouble; Fire, burn; and, cauldron, bubble.
Third Witch:	Scale of dragon, tooth of wolf, Witches' mummy, maw and gulf Of the ravined salt-sea shark, Root of hemlock digged in the dark, Liver of blaspheming Jew, Gall of goat, and slips of yew Slivered in the moon's eclipse, Nose of Turk, and Tartar's lips,

Finger of birth–strangled babe
Ditch–delivered by a drab,
Make the gruel thick and slab:
Add thereto a tiger's chaudron,
For the ingredients of our
    cauldron.

All: Double, double toil and trouble;
Fire, burn; and, cauldron,
    bubble.

William Shakespeare

'Fillet of a fenny snake . . . '
(from *Macbeth*)

'Fillet of a fenny snake,
In the cauldron boil and bake.'
Did the witch intend to say
Boil the liquid quite away,
And go on applying heat
Till the thing is fit to eat?
Then, why not put in that skillet
All the snake not just the fillet?
Which is worse, the poetry
Or the careless recipe?

Roy Fuller

The witch's work song

Two spoons of sherry
Three oz. of yeast,
Half a pound of unicorn,
And God bless the feast.
Shake them in the collander,
Bang them to a chop,
Simmer slightly, snip up nicely,
Jump, skip, hop.
Knit one, knot one, purl two together,
Pip one and pop one and pluck the secret
    feather.

Baste in a mod. oven.
God bless our coven.
Tra–la–la!
Three toads in a jar.
Te–he–he!
Put in the frog's knee.
Peep out of the lace curtain.
There goes the Toplady girl, she's up to no
    good that's certain.
Oh, what a lovely baby!
How nice it would go with gravy.
Pinch the salt,
Turn the malt
With a hey-nonny-nonny and I don't mean
    maybe.

T. H. White

Bewitched

I have heard a lady this night,
  Lissom and jimp and slim,
Calling me – calling me over the heather,
  'Neath the beech boughs dusk and dim.

I have followed a lady this night,
  Followed her far and lone,
Fox and adder and weasel know
  The ways that we have gone.

I sit at my supper 'mid honest faces,
  And crumble my crust and say
Nought in the long–drawn drawl of the voices
  Talking the hours away.

I'll go to my chamber under the gable,
  And the moon will lift her light
In at my lattice from over the moorland
  Hollow and still and bright.

And I know she will shine on a lady of
      witchcraft,
  Gladness and grief to see,
Who has taken my heart with her nimble
      fingers,
  Calls in my dreams to me;

Who has led me a dance by dell and dingle
　　My human soul to win,
Made me a changeling to my own, own
　　　　mother,
　　A stranger to my kin.

Walter de la Mare

The changeling

Mary's mother is tall and fair,
Her father is freckled with ginger hair,
And they live in a house all polished and neat
In the very centre of Riverside Street.

But Mary is dark and thin and wild,
And she doesn't laugh like a human child,
And she doesn't cry like you and me
With tears as salt as the brooding sea.

For when Mary giggles the rattling sound
Is worse than the traffic for miles around;
And the sobs that heave Mary's shoulders high,
Leave her throat parched and her wide eyes dry.

In the classroom Mary works on her own,
And she plays in the playground quite alone.
In church she will not pray or sing,
For she never will join in anything.

It can only be that ten years ago,
In hurtling sleet and blinding snow,
Some dreaming wizards or spiteful elves
Went cradle-swapping to please themselves,

Took the real Mary to join their race
And left their fledgling, in her place,
To grow both beautiful and sly
With power to destroy in her evil eye.

And the only thing both Marys share
Is that they are homesick everywhere.
So sumptuously by the fairies fed,
The one is hungry for human bread.

The other however the heat's turned higher
Is cold for the lack of fairy fire.
And the parents cannot know what is meant
By their daughter's waspish discontent.

Her sulks and tempers are never done,
She's a stock of harsh words for everyone;
While they, dismayed by their puzzling fate,
Go to bed early and get up late.

So now the mother is bent and grey,
And the father sits in his chair all day,
And Riverside Street cannot abide
The slum that their house has become inside.

Shirley Toulson

Fairy things

Grey lichens, mid thy hills of creeping thyme,
Grow like to fairy forests hung with rime;
And fairy money-pots are often found
That spring like little mushrooms out of
    ground,
Some shaped like cups and some in slender trim
Wine-glasses like, that to the very rim
Are filled with little mystic shining seed;
We thought our fortunes promising indeed,
Expecting by and by ere night to find
Money ploughed up of more substantial kind.

    Acres of little yellow weeds,
    The wheat-field's constant blooms,
    That ripen into prickly seeds
    For fairy curry-combs,
    To comb and clean the little things
    That draw their nightly wain;
    And so they scrub the beetle's wings
    Till he can fly again.

And flannel for the beds of the queen
From the soft inside of the shell of the bean,
Where the gipsies down in the lonely dells
Had littered and left the plundered shells.

John Clare

Elves' song

Buz! quoth the blue fly;
  Hum! quoth the bee:
Buz! and Hum! they cry,
  And so do we.
In his ear, in his nose,
  Thus do you see?
He ate the dormouse:
  Else it was he.

                    Ben Jonson

The ancient elf

I am the maker,
The builder, the breaker,
The eagle-winged helper,
The speedy forsaker!

The lance and the lyre,
The water, the fire,
The tooth of oppression,
The lip of desire!

The snare and the wing,
The honey, the sting!
When you seek for me – look
For a different thing.

I, careless and gay,
Never mean what I say,
For my thoughts and my eyes
Look the opposite way!

James Stephens

Elves' dance

By the moon we sport and play,
With the night begins our day:
As we frisk the dew doth fall.
Trip it, little urchins all!
Lightly as the little bee,
Two by two, and three by three.
And about go we, and about go we!

John Lyly

Another elves' dance

Round about, round about
   In a fairy ring-a,
Thus we dance, thus we dance
   And thus we sing-a,
Trip and go, to and fro
   Over this green-a,
All about, in and out,
   For our brave Queen-a.

Unknown

The fairies

Up the airy mountain,
   Down the rushy glen,
We daren't go a–hunting,
   For fear of little men;
Wee folk, good folk,
   Trooping all together;
Green jacket, red cap,
   And white owl's feather!

Down along the rocky shore
   Some make their home,
They live on crispy pancakes
   Of yellow tide–foam;
Some in the reeds
   Of the black mountain–lake,
With frogs for their watch–dogs,
   All night awake.

High on the hill–top
   The old King sits;
He is now so old and grey
   He's nigh lost his wits.
With a bridge of white mist
   Columbkill he crosses,
On his stately journeys
   From Slieveleague to Rosses;
Or going up with music
   On cold starry nights,
To sup with the Queen
   Of the gay Northern Lights.

They stole little Bridget
　For seven years long;
When she came down again
　Her friends were all gone.
They took her lightly back,
　Between the night and morrow,
They thought that she was fast asleep
　But she was dead with sorrow.
They have kept her ever since
　Deep within the lakes,
On a bed of flag-leaves,
　Watching till she wakes.

By the craggy hill-side,
　　Through the mosses bare
They have planted thorn-trees
　　For pleasure here and there.
Is any man so daring
　　As dig one up in spite,
He shall find the thornies set
　　In his bed at night.

Up the airy mountain,
　　Down the rushy glen,
We daren't go a-hunting
　　For fear of little men;
Wee folk, good folk,
　　Trooping all together;
Green jacket, red cap,
　　And white owl's feather!

William Allingham

Goblin revel

In gold and grey, with fleering looks of sin,
I watch them come; by two, by three, by four,
Advancing slow, with loutings they begin
Their woven measure, widening from the
　　door;
While music-men behind are straddling in
With flutes to brisk their feet across the floor,
And jangled dulcimers, and fiddles thin
That taunt the twirling antic through once
　　more.

They pause, and hushed to whispers, steal
  away.
With cunning glances; silent go their shoon
On creakless stairs; but far away the dogs
Bark at some lonely farm: and haply they
Have clambered back into the dusky moon
That sinks beyond the marshes loud with frogs.

Siegfried Sassoon

Mab, the mistress-fairy

This is Mab, the mistress-fairy,
That doth nightly rob the dairy,
And can hurt or help the churning
As she please, without discerning:

She that pinches country wenches
If they rub not clean their benches,
And with sharper nails remembers
When they rake not up their embers;
But if so they chance to feast her,
In a shoe she drops a tester.

This is she that empties cradles,
Takes out children, puts in ladles,
Trains forth midwives in their slumber
With a sieve the holes to number;
And then leads them from her boroughs
Home through ponds and water-furrows.

She can start our franklin's daughters
In their sleep with shrieks and laughters,
And on sweet Saint Anne's night
Feed them with a promised sight,
Some of husbands, some of lovers,
Which an empty dream discovers.

Ben Jonson

Overheard on a saltmarsh

Nymph, nymph, what are your beads?
Green glass, goblin. Why do you stare at them?
Give them me.
                    No.
Give them me. Give them me.
                                No.
Then I will howl all night in the reeds,
Lie in the mud and howl for them.

Goblin, why do you love them so?

They are better than stars or water,
Better than voices of winds that sing,
Better than any man's fair daughter,
Your green glass beads on a silver ring.

Hush I stole them out of the moon.

Give me your beads, I desire them.
                                   No.

I will howl in a deep lagoon
For your green glass beads, I love them so.
Give them me. Give them.
                                   No.

                                   Harold Monro

The fairy queen

Come follow, follow me,
You, fairy elves that be:
Which circle on the green,
Come follow Mab, your queen.
Hand in hand let's dance around,
For this place is fairy ground,

When mortals are at rest,
And snoring in their nest;
Unheard and unespied,
Through keyholes we do glide;
Over tables, stools and shelves,
We trip it with our fairy elves.

On tops of dewy grass
So nimbly do we pass,
The young and tender stalk
Never bends when we do walk;
Yet in the mornings may be seen
Where we the night before have been.

Unknown

The fairies

If you will with Mab find grace,
Set each platter in his place:
Rake the fire up and get
Water in, ere sun be set.
Wash your pails and cleanse your dairies;
Sluts are loathsome to the fairies:
Sweep your house: who does not so,
Mab will pinch her by the toe.

Robert Herrick

The fairies' farewell

Farewell, rewards and fairies,
  Good housewives now may say,
For now foul sluts in dairies
  Do fare as well as they;
And though they sweep their hearths no less
  Than maids were wont to do,
Yet who of late for cleanliness
  Finds sixpence in her shoe?

At morning and at evening both,
  You merry were and glad;
So little care of sleep and sloth
  These pretty ladies had;
When Tom came home from labour,
  Or Ciss to milking rose,
Then merrily went their tabor,
  And nimbly went their toes.

A tell–tale in their company
  They never could endure,
And whoso kept not secretly
  Their mirth was punished sure.
It was a just and Christian deed
  To pinch such black and blue;
Oh, how the Commonwealth doth need
  Such justices as you!

Witness those rings and roundelays
　　Of theirs which yet remain,
Were footed in Queen Mary's days
　　On many a grassy plain.
But since of late Elizabeth
　　And later James came in,
They never danced on any heath
　　As when the time had been.

By which we note the fairies
　　Were of the old profession,
Their songs were Ave Maries,
　　Their dances were procession.
But now alas, they all are dead
　　Or gone beyond the seas,
Or further from religion fled,
　　Or else they take their ease.

Richard Corbet

Fairies' song

You spotted snakes, with double tongue,
  Thorny hedgehogs, be not seen;
Newts, and blind-worms, do no wrong;
  Come not near our fairy queen;
  Philomel, with melody,
  Sing in our sweet lullaby;
Lulla, lulla, lullaby; lulla, lulla, lullaby:
  Never harm, nor spell nor charm,
  Come our lovely lady nigh:
  So, good night, with lullaby.

Weaving spiders, come not here;
  Hence, you long-legged spinners, hence:
Beetles black, approach not near;
  Worm, nor snail, do no offence.
  Philomel, with melody,
  Sing in our sweet lullaby;
Lulla, lulla, lullaby; lulla, lulla, lullaby:
  Never harm, nor spell nor charm,
  Come our lovely lady nigh:
  So, good night, with lullaby.

Hence, away! now all is well:
One, aloof, stand sentinel.

William Shakespeare

Charm on seeing a pixie

Jack o' the lantern, Joan the wad!
Who tickled the maid, and made her mad,
Light me home, the weather's bad.

Unknown

A charm

Thrice toss these oaken ashes in the air;
Thrice sit you mute in this enchanted chair;
Then thrice three times tie up this true love's
   knot,
And murmur soft: 'She will, or she will not.'

Go burn these poisonous weeds in yon blue
   fire,
These screech-owl's fathers and this prickling
   briar,
This cypress gathered at a dead man's grave,
That all your fears and cares an end may have.

Then come, you fairies, dance with me a round;
Melt her hard heart with your melodious
   sound.
In vain are all the charms I can devise;
She has an art to break them with her eyes.

Thomas Campion

Charm for a wart

I wash my hands in this your dish,
Oh man in the moon, do grant my wish,
And come and take away this.

Unknown

70

Charm for an adder bite
(or To Make an adder destroy itself)

Underneath this 'hazelen mot'
There's a braggaty worm, with a speckled
   throat,
Now! Nine double has he.
Now from nine double to eight double,
From eight double, to seven double,
From seven double, to six double,
From six double, to five double,
From five double, to four double,
From four double, to three double,
From three double, to two double,
From two double, to one double,
    Now! No double has he.

Unknown

Charm for the sleeping child

Let the superstitious wife
Near the child's heart lay a knife:
Point be up, and shaft be down;
(While she gossips in the town)
This among other mystic charms
Keeps the sleeping child from harms.

Robert Herrick

Charm for the coming day

In the morning when you rise
Wash your hands, and cleanse your eyes.
Next be sure you have a care,
To disperse the water far.
For as far as that does light,
So far keeps the evil sprite.

Robert Herrick

Two charms to cure hiccups

1

Hiccup, hiccup, go away,
Come again another day:
Hiccup, hiccup, when I bake,
I'll give to you a butter–cake

2

Hiccup, snickup,
Rise up, right up,
Three drops in a cup
Are good for the hiccup.

Unknown

A charm for travellers

Here I am and forth I must:
In Jesus Christ is all my trust.
No wicked thing do me no spite,
Here nor elsewhere, day nor night.
The Holy Ghost and the Trinity
Come betwixt my evil spirit and me.

Unknown

Charm to cure cramp

The Devil is tying a knot in my leg,
Matthew, Mark, Luke and John, unloose it I
    beg:
Crosses three we make to ease us,
Two for the thieves and one for Christ Jesus.

Unknown

Charming

You can sell them for a penny to
your mother

or

You can tie knots for each one
in a piece of string
and plant it at the bottom of your garden
and water it
every morning
that makes them grow under the earth

or

You can have them charmed
if you know a charmer
there are lots in Cornwall you must
leave her a gift and not say thank you
then she will sing
an incantation

or

there is the witches way.
You take a special white round stone
for every one
and put them in a pretty red bag
into the middle of the road –

Don't touch that bag it's got
warts in it

or

If you can find the green toad you
got them from you can
give them back to him if he'll have them

or

You can rub snails on them or slugs
and if that doesn't cure them

you still want them.

Jeni Couzyn

A spell for sleeping

Sweet william, silverweed, sally-my-
  handsome.
Dimity darkens the pittering water.
On gloomed lawns wanders a king's daughter.

Curtains are clouding the casement windows.
A moon-glade smurrs the lake with light.
Doves cover the tower with quiet.

Three owls whit-whit in the withies.
Seven fish in a deep pool shimmer.
The princess moves to the spiral stair.

Slowly the sickle moon mounts up.
Frogs hump under moss and mushroom.
The princess climbs to her high hushed room,

Step by step to her shadowed tower.
Water laps the white lake shore.
A ghost opens the princess's door.

  Seven fish in the sway of the water.
  Six candles for a king's daughter.
  Five sighs for a drooping head.
  Four ghosts to gentle her bed.
  Three owls in the dusk falling.
  Two tales to be telling.
  One spell for sleeping.

Tamarisk, trefoil, tormentil.
Sleep rolls down from the clouded hill.
A princess dreams of a silver pool.

The moonlight spreads, the soft ferns flitter.
Stilled in a shimmering drift of water,
Seven fish dream of a lost king's daughter.

Alastair Reid

Two love-charms

1
You magic power in the skies
who love the rains
make it so that he
no matter how many women he has
will think them all ugly
make him remember me
remember me
this afternoon
when the sun goes to the west

2
New moon
new moon
here I am in your presence
make it so
that only I
may occupy his heart

Tupi Indians, South America

Spells

Norway, Galway, Isle of Skye,
Out of the corner of my left eye
I saw a Chinaman shuffling by,
There's tons of salt in the Caspian Sea,
And that's the spell I made for ME.

William, Elizabeth, George the Third,
Such a funny sound I suddenly heard,
Half a laugh and half a word,
King John started the hullabaloo,
And that's the spell I made for YOU.

Tigers, spiders, American bears,
There was a crocodile crawling up the stairs.
I knelt down and said my prayers,
Hippo–potto–hippopotamus,
And that's the spell I made for US.

Leonard Clark

A spell to destroy life

Listen!
        Now I have come to step over your soul
            (I know your clan)
            (I know your name)
            (I have stolen your spit and buried it
                under earth)
I bury your soul under earth
I cover you over with black rock
I cover you over with black cloth
I cover you over with black slabs
You disappear forever

Your path leads to the
                Black Coffin
                in the hills of the Darkening Land

So let it be for you

The clay of the hills covers you
The black clay of the Darkening Land

Your soul fades away

It becomes blue (colour of despair)
When darkness comes your spirit shrivels
    and dwindles to disappear forever
Listen!

Cherokee Indians, North America

A spell for creation

Within the flower there lies a seed,
Within the seed there springs a tree,
Within the tree there spreads a wood.

In the wood there burns a fire,
And in the fire there melts a stone,
Within the stone a ring of iron.

Within the ring there lies an O
Within the O there looks an eye,
In the eye there swims a sea,

And in the sea reflected sky,
And in the sky there shines the sun,
Within the sun a bird of gold.

Within the bird there beats a heart,
And from the heart there flows a song,
And in the song there sings a word.

In the word there speaks a world,
A world of joy, a world of grief,
From joy and grief there springs my love.

Oh love, my love, there springs a world,
And on the world there shines a sun
And in the sun there burns a fire,

Within the fire consumes my heart
And in my heart there beats a bird,
And in the bird there wakes an eye,

Within the eye, earth, sea and sky,
Earth, sky and sea within an O
Lie like the seed within the flower.

Kathleen Raine

Mean song

Snickles and podes,
Ribble and grodes:
That's what I wish you.

A nox in the groot,
A root in the stoot
And a gock in the forbeshaw, too.

Keep out of sight
For fear that I might
Glom you a gravely snave.

Don't show your face
Around any place
Or you'll get one flack snack in the bave.

Eve Merriam

A traveller's curse after misdirection
(from the Welsh)

May they stumble, stage by stage
On an endless pilgrimage,
Dawn and dusk, mile after mile,
At each and every step, a stile;
At each and every step withal
May they catch their feet and fall;
At each and every fall they take
May a bone within them break:
And may the bone that breaks within
Not be, for variation's sake,
Now rib, now thigh, now arm, now shin,
But always, without fail, THE NECK.

Robert Graves

To the grave with many a curse

Thin in beard, and thick in purse,
Never man beloved worse,
He went to the grave with many a curse:
The Devil and he had both one nurse.

Unknown

Right cheek! left cheek!

Right cheek! left cheek! why do you burn?
Cursed be she that does me any harm;
If she be a maid, let her be staid;
If she be a widow, long let her mourn;
But if it be my own true love – burn, cheek,
    burn!

Unknown

Meet-on-the-Road

'Now, pray, where are you going?' said Meet-on-the-Road.
'To school, sir, to school, sir,' said Child-as-it-Stood.

'What have you in your basket, child?' said Meet-on-the-Road.
'My dinner, sir, my dinner, sir,' said Child-as-it-Stood.

'What have you for dinner, child?' said Meet-on-the-Road.
'Some pudding, sir, some pudding, sir,' said Child-as-it-Stood.

'Oh, then, I pray, give me a share,' said Meet-on-the-Road.
'I've little enough for myself, sir,' said Child-as-it-Stood.

'What have you got that cloak on for?' said Meet-on-the-Road.
'To keep the wind and cold from me,' said Child-as-it-Stood.

'I wish the wind would blow through you,' said Meet-on-the-Road.
'Oh, what a wish! What a wish!' said Child-as-it-Stood.

'Pray, what are those bells ringing for?' said
    Meet–on–the–Road.
'To ring bad spirits home again,' said Child–as–
    it–Stood.

'Oh, then I must be going, child!' said Meet–
    on–the–Road.
'So fare you well, so fare you well,' said Child–
    as–it–Stood.

Unknown

Here lie the beasts

Here lie the beasts of man and here I feast,
The dead man said,
And silently I milk the Devil's breast.
Here spring the silent venoms of his blood,
Here clings the meat to sever from his side.
Hell's in the dust.

Here lies the beast of man and here his angels,
The dead man said,
And silently I milk the buried flowers.
Here drips a silent honey in my shroud,
Here slips the ghost who made of my pale bed
The heaven's house.

Dylan Thomas

The Dark Angel

Dark Angel, with thine aching lust
To rid the world of penitence:
Malicious Angel, who still dost
My soul such subtile violence!

Because of thee, no thought, no thing
Abides for me undesecrate:
Dark Angel, ever on the wing,
Who never reachest me too late!

Through thee, the gracious Muses turn
To Furies, O mine Enemy!
And all the things of beauty burn
With flames of evil ecstasy.

Because of thee, the land of dreams
Becomes a gathering-place of fears:
Until tormented slumber seems
One vehemence of useless tears.

When sunlight glows upon the flowers,
Or ripples down the dancing sea:
Thou, with thy troop of passionate powers,
Beleaguerest, bewilderest me.

Within the breath of autumn woods,
Within the winter silences:
Thy venomous spirit stirs and broods,
O Master of impieties!

The ardour of red flame is thine,
And thine the steely soul of ice:
Thou poisonest the fair design
Of nature, with unfair device.

Thou art the whisper in the gloom,
The hinting tone, the haunting laugh:
Thou art the adorner of my tomb,
The minstrel of mine epitaph.

Do what thou wilt, thou shalt not so,
Dark Angel! triumph over me:
Lonely, unto the Lone I go;
Divine, to the Divinity.

Lionel Johnson

A linnet in Hell

A linnet who had lost her way
Sang on a blackened bough in Hell,
Till all the ghosts remembered well
The trees, the wind, the golden day.

At last they knew that they had died
When they heard music in that land,
And someone there stole forth a hand
To draw a brother to his side.

James Elroy Flecker

The start of a memorable holiday

Good evening, sir. Good evening, ma'am.
  Good evening, little ladies.
From all the staff, a hearty welcome to the
  Hotel Hades.
Oh yes, sir, since you booked your rooms we
  have been taken over
And changed our name – but for the better – as
  you'll soon discover.
Porter, Room 99! Don't worry, sir – just now
  he took
Much bulkier things than bags on his pathetic
  iron hook.
The other room, the children's room? I'm very
  pleased to say
We've put them in the annexe, half a mile across
  the way.
They'll have a nearer view there of the bats'
  intriguing flying,
And you, dear sir and madam, won't be
  troubled by their crying
– Although I'm sure that neither of them's
  frightened of the gloom.
Besides, the maid will try to find a candle for
  their room.

Of course, ma'am, we've a maid there; she's the
    porter's (seventh) wife:
She'll care for these dear children quite as well
    as her own life.
The journey's tired them? Ah, tonight they
    won't be counting sheep!
I'll see they have a nice hot drink before they're
    put to sleep.
Don't be too late yourselves, sir, for the hotel's
    evening meal:
I hope that on the menu will be some roast
    milk–fed veal.
If you'll forgive me, I must stoke the ovens
    right away:
It's going to be (excuse the joke) hell in this
    place today!
Yes, I do all the cooking *and* the getting of the
    meat:
Though we're so far from shops we've usually
    something fresh to eat.
Of course, it isn't always veal, and when the
    school terms start
Joints may get tougher. But our gravy still stays
    full of heart!

Roy Fuller

The ghoul

The gruesome ghoul, the grisly ghoul,
without the slightest noise
waits patiently beside the school
to feast on girls and boys.

He lunges fiercely through the air
as they come out to play,
then grabs a couple by the hair
and drags them far away.

He cracks their bones and snaps their backs
and squeezes out their lungs,
he chews their thumbs like candy snacks
and pulls apart their tongues.

He slices their stomachs and bites their hearts
and tears their flesh to shreds,
he swallows their toes like toasted tarts
and gobbles down their heads.

Fingers, elbows, hands and knees
and arms and legs and feet –
he eats them with delight and ease,
for every part's a treat.

And when the gruesome, grisly ghoul
has nothing left to chew,
he hurries to another school
and waits . . . perhaps for you.

Jack Prelutsky

Song of the ogres

Little fellow, you're amusing,
Stop before you end by losing
   Your shirt:
Run along to Mother, Gus,
Those who interfere with us
   Get hurt.

Honest Virtue, old wives prattle,
Always wins the final battle.
   Dear, Dear!
Life's exactly what it looks,
Love may triumph in the books,
   Not here.

We're not joking, we assure you:
Those who rode this way before you
   Died hard.
What? Still spoiling for a fight?
Well, you've asked for it all right:
   On guard!

Always hopeful, aren't you? Don't be.
Night is falling and it won't be
   Long now:
You will never see the dawn,
You will wish you'd not been born.
   And how!

W. H. Auden

The ogre

In a foul and filthy cavern
where the sun has never shone,
the one-eyed ogre calmly gnaws
a cold and mouldy bone.

He sits in silence in the slime
that fills his fetid home
and notes the nearing footsteps
in the monstrous catacomb.

The one-eyed ogre drools with joy,
his stony heart beats fast,
he knows that for some girl or boy
this day shall be their last.

He wields his ugly cudgel
in a wide and vicious arc,
it swiftly finds his victim
in the deep and deadly dark.

Then down and down and down again
the ogre's blows descend,
to rend, and render senseless,
to speed his victim's end.

So pity those who stumble through
the one-eyed ogre's cave –
that dark abode he calls his home
shall surely be their grave.

Jack Prelutsky

St Newlina's staff

This fig tree is her staff, folks say.
Destroy it not in any way.
Upon it lays a dreadful curse,
Who plucks a leaf will need a hearse.

Unknown

The Horny Goloch

The Horny Goloch is an awesome beast,
Supple and scaly;
It has two horns, and a hantle of feet,
And a forkie tailie.

Unknown

In the orchard

There was a giant by the Orchard Wall
Peeping about on this side and on that,
And feeling in the trees. He was as tall
As the big apple tree, and twice as fat:
His beard poked out, all bristly-black, and there
Were leaves and gorse and heather in his hair.

He held a blackthorn club in his right hand,
And plunged the other into every tree,
Searching for something – You could stand
Beside him and not reach up to his knee,
So big he was – I trembled lest he should
Come trampling, round-eyed, down to where I
    stood.

I tried to get away – But, as I slid
Under a bush, he saw me, and he bent
Down deep at me, and said, *'Where is she hid?'*
I pointed over there, and off he went –

But, while he searched, I turned and simply
  flew
Round by the lilac bushes back to you.

James Stephens

The Sniggle

The Sniggle (often called the Snyle)
Is not a lovely animile.
He has four legs equipped with claws,
Another six with sucker-paws.
When thus he climbs up walls of rock,
You hear his suckers go *plick-plock*.
Plick-plock plick-plock — by night he crawls
On gutter-pipes and roofs and walls.
The Sniggle's is a groujus noise,
Dreaded by all offending boys.

The Sniggle lurks in Woeful Woods
And noses out his favourite foods —
The slow-worm and the blunderbug,
The slurp, the giant hairy slug,
Also that most galooshus dish,
The frozocrumm or finger-fish.

The full-grown adult Snyle (or Sniggle)
Has one long horn which he can wiggle,
Emitting a ferocious bray
With which to terrorize his prey.
When terrorized himself, the Snyle
Secretes a black and fexious bile.
The men who flourished long ago
Beside the River Gallimo
Use it to smear upon their skins
To scare away the gobbolins.
Others, for more artistic ends,
Employed it to surprise their friends
By making abstract wall designs
In flowing and expressive lines.

Noxious as is the Sniggle male,
To see his mate your heart would fail,
For she is squalid, squat and small.
She has no bile, no claws at all;
Her horn is short and will not wiggle,
Her only note a nervous giggle.
She lives on scraps her mate supplies.
I say in short, and none denies,
The female Sniggle is a creature
Without a sole redeeming feature.
So I conclude with jubilation
This sad, this groojus recitation.

James Reeves

The Gombeen

Behind a web of bottles, bales,
Tobacco, sugar, coffin nails
The Gombeen like a spider sits,
Surfeited; and, for all his wits,
As meagre as the tally-board
On which his usuries are scored.

The mountain people come and go
For wool to weave or seed to sow,
White flour to bake a wedding cake,
Red spirits for a stranger's wake.
No man can call his soul his own
Who has the Devil's spoon on loan.

And so behind his web of bales,
Horse halters, barrels, pucaun sails
The Gombeen like a spider sits,
Surfeited; and, for all his wits,
As poor as one who never knew
The treasure of the early dew.

Joseph Campbell

The Demon Manchanda

The two-headed two-body,
the Demon Manchanda
had eyes bigger than his belly.
He walked and talked
right round the world
but every time he opened his mouth
he put his foot in it.

'You're pulling my leg,'
he said to himself.
So he ate his words instead.
I suppose you know the rest:
he went to the window
and threw out his chest.

Michael Rosen

Multikertwigo

I saw the Multikertwigo
Standing on his head,
He was looking at me sideways
And this is what he said:
'Sniddle Iddle Ickle Thwack
Nicki – Nacki – Noo
Biddle – diddle Dicky – Dack
Tickle – tockle – too!
None of this made sense to me,
Maybe it does to you.

Spike Milligan

Dinky

O what's the weather in a Beard?
It's windy there, and rather weird,
And when you think the sky has cleared
    — Why, there is Dirty Dinky.

Suppose you walk out in a Storm,
With nothing on to keep you warm,
And then step barefoot on a Worm
    — Of course, it's Dirty Dinky.

As I was crossing a hot hot Plain,
I saw a sight that caused me pain,
You asked me before, I'll tell you again:
    — It *looked* like Dirty Dinky.

Last night you lay a–sleeping? No!
The room was thirty-five below;
The sheets and blankets turned to snow.
    — He'd got in: Dirty Dinky.

You'd better watch the things you do,
You'd better watch the things you do.
You're part of him; he's part of you
    — *You* may be Dirty Dinky.

Theodore Roethke

'Be a monster'

I am a frightful monster,
My face is cabbage green
And even with my mouth shut
My teeth can still be seen.
My finger-nails are like rats' tails
And very far from clean.

I cannot speak a language
But make a wailing sound.
It could be any corner
You find me coming round.
Then, arms outspread and eyeballs red,
I skim across the ground.

The girls scream out and scatter
From this girl-eating bat.
I usually catch a small one
Because her legs are fat;
Or it may be she's tricked by me
Wearing her grandpa's hat.

Roy Fuller

I am Jojo

I am Jojo
give me the sun to eat.
I am Jojo
give me the moon to suck.

The waters of my mouth
will put out the fires of the sun;
the waters of my mouth
will melt the light of the moon.

Day becomes night,
night becomes day.
I am Jojo
listen to what I say.

Michael Rosen

Glaucopis

John Fane Dingle
    By Rumney Brook
Shot a crop-eared owl,
    For pigeon mistook:

Caught her by the lax wing.
    – She, as she dies,
Thrills his warm soul through
    With her deep eyes.

Corpse–eyes are eerie:
   Tiger–eyes fierce:
John Fane Dingle found
   Owl–eyes worse.

Owl–eyes on night–clouds,
   Constant as Fate:
Owl–eyes in baby's face:
   On dish and plate:

Owl–eyes, without sound.
   – Pale of hue
John died of no complaint,
   With owl–eyes too.

Richard Hughes

Tom Bone

My name is Tom Bone,
I live all alone
In a deep house on Winter Street.
   Through my mud wall
   The wolf–spiders crawl
   And the mole has his beat.

On my roof of green grass
All the day footsteps pass
In the heat and the cold,
   As snug in a bed
   With my name at its head
   One great secret I hold.

Tom Bone, when the owls rise
In the drifting night skies
Do you walk round about?
   All the solemn hours through
   I lie down just like you
   And sleep the night out.

Tom Bone, as you lie there
On your pillow of hair,
What grave thoughts do you keep?
   Tom says, Nonsense and stuff!
   You'll know soon enough.
   Sleep, darling, sleep.

Charles Causley

Enchanter

'Beware! Beware!
His flashing eyes, his floating hair!
Weave a circle round him thrice,
And close your eyes with holy dread,
For he on honey–dew has fed,
And drunk the milk of Paradise.'

Samuel Taylor Coleridge

The King of Terrors

'Prepare to meet the King of Terrors,' cried
To prayerless Want, his plunderer ferret–eyed:
'I am the King of Terrors,' Want replied.

Ebenezer Elliot

Sorcerer

Well now, what shall be
Today's magic? . .
Let me see.

Shall I build a castle in Spain –
Stone stairways, flight upon flight;
Bastions, fantastical turrets . . . and at twilight
Unbuild it again?

Shall I launch a ship to the seas,
Silk-sailed with riggings of gold,
To fathom some distant, strange, untold
    Hesperides?

Shall I shatter a forest of gloom
With a Palace, where torches and candles
  respond
To thousands of mirrors, room beyond
    Glittering room?

Shall I summon beasts to be born,
And birds contrived by curious tricks
Of breeding – gryphon and wyvern, phoenix
    And unicorn?

Or command a tempest, to roar
Through heaven and ocean – raging storms
And wild tramontanas, in force and forms
    Not loosed before?

Shall I darken day; the sun
Wrenched from his course; his planets hurled
Headlong down space; the world
    And it's life undone? . .

        No! no! – let it be
        Some gentler magic.
        Let me see.

        Clive Sansom

The magician's attic

The woodwork's musty as the russet smell of
   old burnt toast and almonds.
The feather-hands
Of the falcon-clock have stopped.
                  There are no sounds,
Except the old creaking rocking-throne that
   stands
In a corner (still rocking, for kings and queens
   have ghosts called Histories).
                        Ends
Of cowboys' cattle-brands
Hang on a wall.
              The table's one leg bends
Like a toad-stool stalk.
              The magician never mends
His old things. He never sends
Them to auction-sales, bazaars or jumble-
   sales. Indeed, he intends
To keep his attic cluttered with peaceful
      rubbish,
   quieter than islands.
The air is still with the dust of grated
   diamonds.
The feather-hands
Of the falcon-clock have stopped.

                    He finds
Old things are good for games of memories,
     and sometimes he stands
For hours staring at wands –
For this is where he keeps them, old,
     splintered, broken, worn–out wizard wands.

                              Harold Massingham

Oh! my name is John Wellington Wells

Oh! my name is John Wellington Wells –
I'm a dealer in magic and spells,
     In blessings and curses,
     And ever–filled purses,
In prophecies, witches, and knells!
If you want a proud foe to 'make tracks' –
If you'd melt a rich uncle in wax –
     You've but to look in
     On our resident Djinn,
Number seventy, Simmery Axe.

We've a first-class assortment of magic;
    And for raising a posthumous shade
With effects that are comic or tragic,
    There's no cheaper house in the trade.
Love-philtre – we've quantities of it;
    And for knowledge if any one burns,
We keep an extremely small prophet, a prophet
    Who brings us unbounded returns:
        For he can prophesy
        With a wink of his eye,
        Peep with security
        Into futurity,
        Sum up your history,
        Clear up a mystery,
        Humour proclivity
        For a nativity.
        With mirrors so magical,
        Tetrapods tragical,
        Bogies spectacular,
        Answers oracular,
        Facts astronomical,
        Solemn or comical,
        And, if you want it, he
Makes a reduction on taking a quantity!
        Oh!
If any one anything lacks,
He'll find it all ready in stacks,
      If he'll only look in
      On the resident Djinn,
Number seventy, Simmery Axe!

                    W. S. Gilbert

Robin Good-fellow

From Oberon, in fairy–land,
   The king of ghosts and shadows there,
Mad Robin I, at his command,
   Am sent to view the night–sports here.
     What revel rout
     Is kept about,
In every corner where I go,
     I will oversee,
     And merry be,
And make good sport, with ho, ho, ho!

More swift than lightning can I fly
  About this airy welkin soon,
And, in a minute's pace, descry
  Each thing that's done below the moon,
    There's not a hag
    Or ghost shall wag,
  Or cry, ware goblins! where I go:
    But Robin I
    Their feats will spy,
And send them home, with ho, ho, ho!

Whenever such wanderers I meet,
  As from their night-sports they trudge
    home;
With counterfeiting voice I greet
  And call them on, with me to roam
    Through woods, through lakes,
    Through bogs, through brakes;
  Or else, unseen, with them I go,
    All in the nick
    To play some trick
And frolic it, with ho, ho, ho!

Sometimes I meet them like a man;
  Sometimes, an ox, sometimes, a hound;
And to a horse I turn me can;
  To trip and trot about them round.
    But, if, to ride,
    My back they stride,
  More swift than wind away I go,
    Over hedge and lands,
    Through pools and ponds
I whirry, laughing, ho, ho, ho!

When men do traps and engines set
　　In loop-holes, where the vermin creep,
Who from their folds and houses, get
　　Their ducks and geese, and lambs and sheep:
　　　　I spy the gin,
　　　　And enter in,
　　And seem a vermin taken so;
　　　　But when they there
　　　　Approach me near,
　　I leap out laughing, ho, ho, ho!

By wells and rills, in meadows green,
　　We nightly dance our hey-day guise;
And to our fairy king, and queen,
　　We chant our moonlight minstrelsies.
　　　　When larks begin to sing,
　　　　Away, thus, we fling;
　　And babes new born steal as we go,
　　　　And else in bed,
　　　　We leave instead,
　　And wend us laughing, ho, ho, ho!

From hag-bred Merlin's time have I
　　Thus nightly revelled to and fro:
And for my pranks men call me by
　　The name of Robin Good-fellow.
　　　　Fiends, ghosts, and sprites,
　　　　Who haunt the nights,
　　The hags and goblins do me know;
　　　　And beldames old
　　　　My feats have told;
　　So *Vale, Vale*; ho, ho, ho!

Unknown

A meeting

When George began to climb all unawares
He saw a horrible face at the top of the stairs.

The rats came tumbling down the planks,
Pushing past without a word of thanks.

The rats were thin, the stairs were tall,
But the face at the top was the worst of all.

It wasn't the ghost of his father or mother.
When they are laid there's always another.

It wasn't the ghost of the people he knew.
It was worse than this, shall I tell you who?

It was himself, oh what a disgrace.
And soon they were standing face to face.

At first they pretended neither cared
But when they met they stood and stared.

One started to smile and the other to frown,
And one moved up and the other moved down.

But which emerged and which one stays,
Nobody will know till the end of his days.

George D. Painter

Midnight wood

Dark in the wood the shadows stir:
   What do you see? —
Mist and moonlight, star and cloud,
Hunchback shapes that creep and crowd
   From tree to tree.

Dark in the wood a thin wind calls:
   What do you hear? —
Frond and fern and clutching grass
Snigger at you as you pass,
   Whispering fear.

Dark in the wood a river flows:
   What does it hide? —
Otter, water–rat, old tin can,
Bones of fish and bones of a man
   Drift in its tide.

Dark in the wood the owlets shriek:
   What do they cry? —
Choose between the wood and river;
Who comes here is lost forever,
   And must die!

Raymond Wilson

The magic wood

The wood is full of shining eyes,
The wood is full of creeping feet,
The wood is full of tiny cries:
You must not go to the wood at night!

I met a man with eyes of glass
And a finger as curled as the wriggling worm,
And hair all red with rotting leaves,
And a stick that hissed like a summer snake.

He sang me a song in backwards words,
And drew me a dragon in the air.
I saw his teeth through the back of his head,
And a rat's eyes winking from his hair.

He made me a penny out of a stone,
And showed me the way to catch a lark
With a straw and a nut and a whispered word
And a pennorth of ginger wrapped up in a leaf.

He asked me my name, and where I lived;
I told him a name from my Book of Tales;
He asked me to come with him into the wood
And dance with the Kings from under the hills.

But I saw that his eyes were turning to fire;
I watched the nails grow on his wriggling hand;
And I said my prayers, all out in a rush,
And found myself safe on my father's land.

Oh, the wood is full of shining eyes,
The wood is full of creeping feet,
The wood is full of tiny cries:
You must not go to the wood at night!

Henry Treece

Queer things

'Very, very queer things have been happening
    to me
    In some of the places where I've been.
I went to the pillar-box this morning with a
        letter
    And a hand came out and took it in.

'When I got home again, I thought I'd have
   A glass of spirits to steady myself;
And I take my bible oath, but that bottle and
      glass
   Came a–hopping down off the shelf.

'No, no, I says, I'd better take no spirits,
   And I sat down to have a cup of tea;
And blowed if my old pair of carpet-slippers
   Didn't walk across the carpet to me!

'So I took my newspaper and went into the
      park,
   And looked round to see no one was near,
When a voice right out of the middle of the
      paper
   Started reading the news bold and clear!

'Well, I guess there's some magician out to help
      me,
   So perhaps there's no need for alarm;
And if I manage not to anger him,
   Why should he do me any harm?'

James Reeves

The intruder

Two–boots in the forest walks,
Pushing through the bracken stalks.

Vanishing like a puff of smoke,
Nimbletail flies up the oak.

Longears helter–skelter shoots
Into his house among the roots.

At work upon the highest bark,
Tapperbill knocks off to hark.

Painted–wings through sun and shade
Flounces off along the glade.

Not a creature lingers by,
When clumping Two–boots comes to pry.

James Reeves

The empty house

Where the lone wind on the hilltop
Shakes the thistles as it passes,
Stirs the quiet-ticking grasses
That keep time outside the door,
Stands a house that's grey and silent;
No one lives there any more.

Wending through the broken windows,
Every season and its weather
Whisper in those rooms together:
Summer's warm and wandering rains
Rot the leaves of last year's autumn,
Warp the floors that winter stains.

In a papered hall a clock-shape,
Dim and pale on yellowed flowers,
Still remains where rang the hours
Of a clock that's lost and gone.
And the fading ghost keeps no-time
On the wall it lived upon.

On a stairway where no footsteps
Stir the dusty sunlight burning
Sit the patient shadows turning
Speechless faces to the wall
While they hear the silent striking
Of that no-clock in the hall.

'Dawn of no-time! Noon of no-time!'
Cries the phantom echo chiming,
And the shadows, moving, miming,
Slowly shift before the light.
But no eye has seen their motion
When the clock says, 'No-time night!'

No eye has seen them dancing
In their blackness fell and bright,
To a silent tune
In the dark of the moon
When the clock sings no-time night.

Russell Hoban

Haunted

Black hill
black hall
all still
owl's grey cry
edges shrill
castle night.

Woken eye
round in fright;
what lurks walks
in castle rustle?

Hand cold
held hand
the moving roving
urging thing;
dreamed margin

voiceless
noiseless
HEARD
feared
a ghost passed

black hill
black hall
all still
owl's grey cry
edges shrill
castle night.   *William Mayne*

The old stone house

Nothing on the grey roof, nothing on the
   brown,
Only a little greening where the rain drips
   down;
Nobody at the window, nobody at the door,
Only a little hollow which a foot once wore;
But still I tread on tiptoe, still tiptoe on I go,
Past nettles, porch, and weedy well, for oh, I
   know
A friendless face is peering, and a clear still eye
Peeps closely through the casement as my step
   goes by.

Walter de la Mare

So ghostly then the girl came in

So ghostly then the girl came in
I never saw the turnstile twist
Down where the orchard trees begin
Lost in a reverie of mist.

And in the windless hour between
The last of daylight and the night,
When fields give up their ebbing green
And two bats interweave their flight,

I saw the turnstile glimmer pale
Just where the orchard trees begin,
But watching was of no avail,
Invisibly the girl came in.

I took one deep breath of the air
And lifted up my heavy heart;
It was not I who trembled there
But my immortal counterpart.

I knew that she had come again
Up from the orchard through the stile,
Without a sigh to tell me when,
Though I was watching all the while.

Robert Hillyer

The haunted house

Some dreams we have are nothing else but
    dreams,
Unnatural, and full of contradictions;
Yet others of our most romantic schemes
Are something more than fictions.

It might be only on enchanted ground;
It might be merely by a thought's expansion;
But in the spirit, or the flesh, I found
An old deserted mansion.

A residence for woman, child, and man,
A dwelling-place – and yet no habitation;
A house – but under some prodigious ban
Of excommunication.

Unhinged the iron gates half open hung,
Jarred by the gusty gales of many winters,
That from its crumbled pedestal had flung
One marble globe in splinters.

No dog was at the threshold, great or small;
No pigeon on the roof – no household
    creature –
No cat demurely dozing on the wall –
Not one domestic feature.

No human figure stirred, to go or come,
No face looked forth from shut or open
   casement;
No chimney smoked – there was no sign of
   home
From parapet to basement.

With shattered panes the grassy court was
   starred;
The time-worn coping-stone had tumbled
   after!
And through the ragged roof the sky shone,
   barred
With naked beam and rafter.

Over all there hung a shadow and a fear;
A sense of mystery the spirit daunted,
And said, as plain as whisper in the ear,
The place is haunted!

Thomas Hood

Three Ghostesses

There were three ghostesses
Sitting on postesses
Eating buttered toastesses
And greasing their fistesses
Right up to their wristesses.
Weren't they beastesses
To make such feastesses!   *Unknown*

Haunted

Through the imponderable twilight tumbles
    A fuzzy mass, uncertain at the edges.
This, so they tell me, is the ghost that
  grumbles,
    The spectre that goes backwards through
      the hedges,

The goblin garrulous but rarely witty,
    The harmless phantom and the wraith
      endearing,
That hops around and sings a tuneless ditty
    And interrupts himself with bursts of
      cheering;

A spirit fairly lovable, and decent.
    Some say he is the shade of Charles the
      Martyr;
Others incline to a demise more recent,
    Claiming he is a Mr Eustace Carter,

A man who flourished here in eighteen-fifty
    And fell into a pond while trapping
      rabbits.
At all events, although a trifle shifty,
    The spectre has few irritating habits,

Never comes after dark, but in the twilight,
    And rarely frightens people, or not badly,
But sits in summer evenings on the skylight,
    Scratching himself, and singing, rather
        sadly.

R. P. Lister

The wandering spectre

Woe's me, woe's me,
The acorn's not yet fallen from the tree
That's to grow the wood,
That's to make the cradle,
That's to rock the bairn,
That's to grow a man,
That's to lay me.

Unknown

The return

The key turns in the lock,
And I enter my room.
I can hear the solemn clock
Being bold in the gloom.

Through the dark pane
Comes the moon's light,
But it does not explain
The secret way of night.

Only strange shapes
I can see:
The evening drapes
Rooms with black sorcery.

Pausing for light, I can hear
The clock, in the gloom,
Talking to the queer
Ghost in my room.

Clifford Dyment

A room bewitched

In the dark, dark wood, there was
  a dark, dark house,
And in that dark, dark house, there was
  a dark, dark room,
And in that dark, dark room, there was
  a dark, dark cupboard,
And in that dark, dark cupboard, there was
  a dark, dark shelf,
And on that dark, dark shelf, there was
  a dark, dark box,
And in that dark, dark box, there was a . . .

Unknown

Old Mother Laidinwool

Old Mother Laidinwool had nigh twelve
    months been dead.
She heard the hops was doing well, an' so
    popped up her head,
For said she: 'The lads I've picked with when I
    was young and fair,
They're bound to be at hopping and I'm bound
    to meet 'em there!'

> *Let me up and go*
> *Back to the work I know, Lord!*
> *Back to the work I know, Lord!*
> *For it's dark where I lie down, My Lord!*
> *An' it's dark where I lie down.*

Old Mother Laidinwool, she give her bones a
    shake,
An' trotted down the churchyard–path as fast as
    she could make.
She met the Parson walking, but she says to
    him, says she:
'Oh don't let no one trouble for a poor old
    ghost like me!'

'Twas all a warm September an' the hops had
   flourished grand.
She saw the folks get into 'em with stockin's on
   their hands;
An' none of 'em was foreigners but all which
   she had known,
And old Mother Laidinwool she blessed 'em
   every one.

She saw her daughters picking an' their children
   them–beside,
An' she moved among the babies an' she stilled
   'em when they cried.
She saw their clothes was bought, not begged,
   an' they was clean an' fat,
An' Old Mother Laidinwool she thanked the
   Lord for that.

Old Mother Laidinwool she waited on all day
Until it come too dark to see an' people went
   away –
Until it come too dark to see an' lights began to
   show,
An' old Mother Laidinwool she hadn't where
   to go.

Old Mother Laidinwool she give her bones a
    shake,
An' trotted back to churchyard–mould as fast as
    she could make.
She went where she was bidden to an' there laid
    down her ghost . . .
An' the Lord have mercy on you in the Day you
    need it most!

    Let me in again,
    Out of the wet an' rain, Lord!
    Out of the wet an' rain, Lord!
    For it's best as You shall say, My Lord!
    An' it's best as You shall say!

Rudyard Kipling

The visitor

A crumbling churchyard, the sea and the moon;
The waves had gouged out grave and bone;
A man was walking, late and alone . . .

He saw a skeleton on the ground;
A ring on a bony finger he found.

He ran home to his wife and gave her the ring.
'Oh, where did you get it?' He said not a thing.

'It's the loveliest ring in the world,' she said,
As it glowed on her finger. They slipped off to
  bed.

At midnight they woke. In the dark outside,
'Give me my ring!' a chill voice cried.

'What was that, William? What did it say?'
'Don't worry, my dear. It'll soon go away.'

'I'm coming!' A skeleton opened the door.
'Give me my ring!' It was crossing the floor.

'What was that, William? What did it say?'
'Don't worry, my dear. It'll soon go away.'

'I'm reaching you now! I'm climbing the bed.'
The wife pulled the sheet right over her head.

It was torn from her grasp and tossed in the air:
'I'll drag you out of bed by the hair!'

'What was that, William? What did it say?'
'Throw the ring through the window!
  THROW IT AWAY!'

She threw it. The skeleton leapt from the sill,
And into the night it clattered downhill,
Fainter . . . and fainter . . . Then all was still.

Ian Serraillier

Alone in the dark

She has taken out the candle,
She has left me in the dark;
From the window not a glimmer,
From the fireplace not a spark.

I am frightened as I'm lying
All alone here in my bed,
And I've wrapped the clothes as closely
As I can around my head.

But what is it makes me tremble?
And why should I fear the gloom?
I am certain there is nothing
In the corners of the room.

When the candle burned so brightly,
I could see them every one;
Are they changed to something fearful,
Only just because it's gone?

Though I speak, and no one answers,
In the quiet of the night,
Though I look, and through the blackness
Cannot see one gleam of light;

Still I know there's One who seeth
In the night as in the day,
For to Him the darkness dreary
Is as bright as noontide ray.

And perhaps while I am trying
How my foolish face to hide,
There is one of His good angels
Standing watching at my side.

Then I'll turn and sleep more soundly,
When one little prayer I've prayed;
For there's nothing in the darkness
That should make a child afraid.

Unknown

The dark

I feared the darkness as a boy;
And if at night I had to go
Upstairs alone I'd make a show
Of carrying on with those below
A dialogue of shouts and 'whats?'
So they'd be sure to save poor Roy
Were he attacked by vampire bats.

Or thugs or ghosts. But far less crude
Than criminal or even ghost
Behind a curtain or a post
Was what I used to dread the most —
The always-unseen bugaboo
Of black-surrounded solitude.
I dread it still at sixty-two.

Roy Fuller

The Longest Journey in the World

'Last one into bed
has to switch out the light.'
It's just the same every night.
There's a race.
I'm ripping off my trousers and shirt,
he's kicking off his shoes and socks.

'My sleeve's stuck.'
'This button's too big for its button–hole.'
'Have you hidden my pyjamas?'
'Keep your hands off mine.'

If you win
you get where it's safe
before the darkness comes –
but if you lose
if you're last
you know what you've got coming up is
the journey from the light switch to your bed.
It's the Longest Journey in the World.

'You're last tonight,' my brother says.
And he's right.

There is nowhere so dark
as that room in the moment
after I've switched out the light.

There is nowhere so full of dangerous things,
things that love dark places,
things that breathe only when you breathe
and hold their breath when I hold mine.

So I have to say:
'I'm not scared.'
That face, grinning in the pattern on the wall,
isn't a face –
'I'm not scared.'
That prickle on the back of my neck
is only the label on my pyjama jacket –
'I'm not scared.'
That moaning–moaning is nothing
but water in a pipe –
'I'm not scared.'

Everything's going to be just fine
as soon as I get into that bed of mine.
Such a terrible shame
it's always the same
it takes so long
it takes so long
it takes so long
to get there.

From the light switch
to my bed
it's the Longest Journey in the World.

Michael Rosen

Prayer for a night safe from ghosts, sprites and witches

Let no lamenting cries, nor doleful tears
Be heard all night within, nor yet without;
Nor let false whispers, breeding hidden fears,
Break gentle sleep with misconceived doubt.
Let no deluding dreams, nor dreadful sights,
Make sudden sad affrights;
Nor let house-fires, nor lightning's helpless
   harms,
Nor let the Puck, nor other evil sprites,
Nor let mischievous witches with their charms,
Nor let hobgoblins, names whose sense we see
   not,
Fray us with things that be not.
Let not the screech-owl nor the stork be heard,
Nor the night raven that still deadly yells;
Nor damned ghosts, called up with mighty
   spells,
Nor grisly vultures, make us once affeared;
Nor let unpleasant choir of frogs still croaking
Make us to wish their choking.
Let none of these their dreary accents sing:
Nor let the woods them answer, nor their
   echoes ring.

Edmund Spenser

Even on Hallowe'en . . . God is near

I will not fear,
For God is near
Through the dark night,
As in the light;
And while I sleep,
Safe watch will keep.
Even on Hallowe'en
At revels unseen,
Why should I fear
When God is near?

Unknown

Index of titles

Index of authors

Acknowledgments

The editors and publishers wish to thank the following for giving permission to include in this anthology material which is their copyright. If we have inadvertently omitted to acknowledge anyone we should be most grateful if this could be brought to our attention for correction at the first opportunity.

Patricia Ayres for 'Mean Song' from *There Is No Rhyme for Silver* by Eve Merriam. Copyright © 1962 by Eve Merriam. Reprinted by permission of the author. All rights reserved.

George Allen and Unwin for 'Spell of Creation' from *Collected Poems* by Kathleen Raine.

Associated Book Publishers Limited for 'The Bird of Night' from *The Lost World* by Randall Jarrell (Eyre and Spottiswoode).

A & C Black Limited and Greenwillow Books (a division of William Morrow & Co) for 'The Ghoul' and 'The Ogre' from *Nightmares* by Jack Prelutsky. Copyright © 1976 by Jack Prelutsky.

Alan Bold for 'The Malfeasance' by Alan Bold.

Jonathan Cape Limited and the executors of the W.H. Davies estate for 'This Night' from *The Complete Poems of W.H. Davies*.

Collins Publishers for 'The Witch's Work Song' from *The Sword in the Stone* by T.H. White.

Curtis Brown Limited, London, and Pauline Clarke for 'All Hallowe'en' © Pauline Clarke 1962.

J.M. Dent and Sons Limited for 'The Return' from *Straight or Curly* by Clifford Dyment.

André Deutsch Limited for 'Nasty Night', 'Fillet of a Fenny Snake', 'Be a monster' and 'The Dark' from *Poor Roy* by Roy Fuller; for 'The Start of a Memorable Holiday' from *Seen Grandpa Lately* by Roy Fuller; for 'The Demon Manchanda' from *Wouldn't you like to know* by Michael Rosen; and for 'I am Jojo' and 'The Longest Journey in the World' from *You Can't Catch Me* by Michael Rosen.

Trevor Dickinson for 'Hallowe'en' by John Kitching.